# The Pied Piper

Written by Gill Budgell
Illustrated by Tamsin Hinrichsen

# rat

# man

# ran

# hill

# pit

# Talk about the story

Ask your child these questions:

**1** Why were the people in the town upset?

**2** Where did the Pied Piper lead the rats to?

**3** How did the Pied Piper lead the rats away?

**4** How did the townspeople feel when the Pied Piper led the rats away?

**5** How would you have solved the problem of the rats?

**6** Have you ever played a pipe or a recorder?

Can your child retell the story using their own words?